TIME

HEALS

Teri Miller
&
Rosanne Lombardo Heaton

Table of Contents

Dedication

This book is dedicated to all those beautiful souls who have taken that reflective look inward and found the glimpse of what Spirit is all about. It is because of the Oneness of spirit that any of us are able to have the vision to co-create and share with each other, to interact during this and the other many lifetimes here on Earth and beyond. To those who shine their lights brightly, showing the way for others, otherwise referred to as "Lightworkers" or visionaries, this book is dedicated to you for teaching us, inspiring us and holding us up to the light.

We would also like to dedicate this book to the "Electric Company" -- that wonderful spiritual group of seven who took a leap of faith and eagerly embraced this healing modality, allowing Spirit to work in miraculous ways with healing and visions. You are truly remarkable!

Thank you to our spiritual gurus -- those we have learned from and been inspired by in this lifetime. Specifically, Teri would like to thank Nicole Gans Singer for her love and support and for bringing the message from the Masters that one day she would be a healer along with numerous other messages that inspired the quest for more. She would also like to thank Joseph

LoBrutto III for helping her to open up to the spirit guides, The Healers.

Rosanne would like to thank her Archangels for always prodding her forward and for being so patient when life had gotten in the way so many times. Also for those times when she questioned her own faith and spiritual purpose because of all the trials and tribulations experienced in life. Rosanne had been told numerous times that the Angels, when channeled, were holding scrolls in their arms, which represent all of the books she is "yet" to write. This project has propelled her forward with confidence and removed any fear of inadequacy or inability. Rosanne wishes to thank her husband Jimmy for his love, patience and confidence in her projects; her parents for their love and support and for pushing her hard to be confident, goal-oriented and to complete her education; and lastly heartfelt thanks to her Grandmother Anna, who is long deceased in this lifetime but has said numerous times that they have been together before in many lifetimes and that she is a Way-Shower and she is meant to write, so just do it already. Thank you for the push Grandma.

Acknowledgements

We would like to acknowledge some of the people responsible for making this book a reality. First, we are both -- Teri and Rosanne -- so very grateful to have found each other and knew very early in our relationship that we would create something very powerful to bring forth to the world. Without the hard work, sitting at the computer sometimes for hours on end, this would not have become a reality.

Next, we want to thank the Electric Company of seven beautiful souls who committed to five days of receiving the intense healing energy of TIME and gave feedback and verification.

Thank you Ana Borja, Carolina Ferreira de Eidson, Gail Zimmerman, Joanne Nault, Karen Ebenhack, Rosanne Lombardo Heaton and Christina.

As the authors, we would also like to thank those in our lives who "allowed" us the time necessary to do the footwork in putting the book together. Thank you to Tazzie and Gizmo whose water and food bowl sometimes got a little lower than you like, and to Jimmy Heaton for sharing your wife's time to this project as well as Maggie and Kiki who maybe missed out on some daily snuggling.

We would like to thank Peter Davis for his creativity

in designing our cover artwork and his mother, Lisa Jo Davis for her contribution.

A very special thank you goes out to Jennifer Schaffer who saved our hides at the last minute with graphics (whew) and to Sabrina Elizabeth Canillas for her inspiration.

Foreword

To everything, there is a season, a time for every purpose under Heaven. Ecclesiastes 3:1 of the Bible.

Everything has a season and we all understand that nothing on Earth lasts forever. God has appointed a season for everything, therefore seasons begin and end. Life begins and ends. There are seasons for gestation, childhood, youth, middle-age and old-age.

Time therefore indicates a point in time in your life. Conceptually, time in Heaven holds no comparison to Earth time as our time here is considered linear. It has been said that with any given season there is a point in time whereby God has ordained everything to happen.

Humans are creatures of time and we are always preoccupied with it. We count the seconds, minutes, hours, days, months and years. We tick off days on our calendars and we even wear watches to keep account of our time. The concept of time has been a problem for philosophers and biblical scholars alike, and we will not discuss in great detail how time is employed in the Divine schematic as we don't believe there is a proper way to explain it.

We have heard it described by many Angels

that a life-time on Earth is like the blink of an eye in Heaven and what we have learned is that Heaven is timeless.

The TIME Healing modality that we are about to talk about might be more simplistic to understand when you factor in that our Archangels, Healers and Ascended Masters have the capability to be with everyone at any given time, wherever and whenever they are needed or called upon. Therefore, TIME healing crosses the divide of space and time as we know and understand it.

TIME stands for "Theocentric Interactive Magnetic Energy." This is a healing modality that was inspired by the Archangels and a collective of Spirit Guides called The Healers. The healer who has been attuned to TIME is totally connected with Spirit Guides, Archangels and Ascended Masters work though the receiver using the healers physical body as a vessel to dispense healing energy to the receiver. So, how does it work?

In distance healing, the healers calls on the Spirit Guides, Angels and Masters for guidance and then connects to the higher self of the person receiving the healing. A clearing of the auric field is then done followed by a scan of the auric field, which allows us to look for any energetic imbalances or blockages in the chakras. Once these are found, the energy is drawn from the healer's hands to the receiver and the experience can only be described as energy being pulled by a magnet. All of the chakras are cleared and aligned using this method. In a hands-on healing, the methodology is the same although we have been told the experience is different and the healing energy appears to be a bit more intense.

At the end of the session the healer then asks the Angels, Masters and Guides if there are any messages that need to be passed along to the receiver of the healing. Since the healing is interactive, there is a specific set of instructions for the person receiving the healing. This will be outlined in detail in chapter seven.

A Course in Miracles says that God doesn't help us out in times of trouble because He sees no need; meaning He only sees love and perfection and not the illusion of lack or problems in earthly life. God does send helper's when we think we are in trouble and the Angels have said that we would not 'need them' if we stayed fully aware of love's presence at all times and in all situations. The Angels are God's heavenly assistants who help us out whether we call for them or not.

God is everywhere and the Divine is within you and me. In the consciousness of Oneness and our spiritual connection, the Divine light in me acknowledges the Divine light in you. Namaste

TIME

HEALS

18

Chapter 1

THE STORY OF TIME

Once upon a time, a seeker of the light called out to the darkness, knowing without knowing that if she could get beyond the darkness -- beyond the vast unknown -- beyond the illusion of separation and individuality that she would find herself once again. Her real self, not the shell she inhabited while she walked on planet Earth.

Thus, she set about inquiring of those who said they knew the way, those who would tell the secrets IF....and she listened and she read and she prayed and she chanted and she immersed herself in her one goal -- finding the oneness. Eventually, a still, small voice broke through and the message was very clear: drop the crutches. You see, the seeker thought the answers were "out there" somewhere. She had forgotten what she came here for. She thought this life was all about doing because that had been the focus of everything she had heard and read. Do this, don't do that. Do it this way and not that way. Chant this first and then this and then say this many prayers -- and so she did all this without hesitation because she felt that in doing so, she would be led to the oneness.

The seeker spent almost half her lifetime here studying, collecting information, praying, performing rituals, following and using the crutches she thought she needed to be able to walk what she was sure was a never ending trail that would lead her to the oneness. Sometimes she could feel she was on the brink of a major knowing moment and the excitement would build, only to find that she was too scared to put down the crutches and move forward toward the light.

Over these many years, the seeker learned that if she took time to be quiet and still her mind, she could hear the answers she so longed for. She met her spirit guides. She became closer to the Archangels and could recognize when they were speaking to her and she could hear their messages. The messages that came through to her during these meditations taught her about the great love that Spirit has for her and for all of humanity. They taught her of the oneness and showed her how we are all a part of Spirit, that there is no separation.

Her spirit guides were a collective of five, two masculine energies, two feminine energies and one collective within the nucleus. Eventually, they revealed who they were but chose to be referred to as the collective known as The Healers. The seeker had been told over and over at various times that she had great healing ability, which

The Healers confirmed and assured her that it was due to her willingness to be used as a vessel for Spirit to flow energy through her. They also cleared out many blocks from her emotional vibration, things that had transpired this lifetime and taught her about the importance of forgiveness in the healing process.

One day as the seeker was meditating and asking for guidance, the Healers informed her that she was to begin a new healing adventure. The seeker had learned many healing methods in this lifetime, constantly studying the nature of the healing and how it came to be. However, this was different, she was informed. This method would require the person being healed to participate along with the healer; that is, it would be interactive, not passive. It would require a strong connection with Spirit on the part of the healer. It would require a deep understanding that we are all one, thus dropping the illusion of separation. To be a healer meant that you were willing to forego any identity with the ego and only participate from the spiritual fifth dimension, allowing the higher self to communicate with the higher self of the one being administered the healing energy. To take this spiritual healing journey meant a commitment to a daily regimen of clearing oneself of any lower vibrational energy. It involved constantly learning and receiving downloads of information from Spirit as well as renewal via attunements to the healing energy.

The seeker was given a name for this healing method. It was to be called TIME, an acronym for Theocentric Interactive Magnetic Energy. As the seeker received the download of information regarding this method, she was instructed to write out the instructions pertaining to both receiving and giving the healing. The seeker continued to receive attunements daily until she was told to begin using the healing method on others.

One of the agreements on the part of the one being healed is to hold another person in their thoughts while they are receiving the healing, someone who would benefit from receiving love and light in their life as well -- a gift if you will, to pass on once the healing is received.

Immediately upon hearing this requirement, the seeker knew who she was to give this wonderful loving gift to. She contacted her counterpart with whom she had connected along her spiritual journey -- someone with whom there was such an instant soul connection that they both knew they had done this dance before in many lifetimes. They were both healers, thus they knew they had contracted to come here in this lifetime at this particular time to do just that. Once the method was taught to her partner, they both received even more downloads of information and messages and were led to then take this out into the world for the benefit of all.

What follows in the pages of this book is the information from those downloads -- the specific method of performing the healing, of receiving the healing, information about the chakras, about clearing auras, and about channeling messages from Spirit to the recipients of this wonderful healing energy.

May you be blessed from this knowledge and may you find this information useful in your lives.

Namaste

Chapter 2

THE ONENESS

Dr. Wayne Dyer, one of the most well-known and beloved teachers and spiritual mentors of modern time grasped the concept of Oneness and spoke of it often. So have other great leaders such as Paramahansa Yogananda, Deepak Chopra, Lee Carroll, Eckhart Tolle, Maya Angelou, and the list could go on.

We will try to explain it as we were shown by Spirit to help us understand it. Our physical world on Earth is all about contrasts, or opposites. The concept of up would not make sense if there was no down. How would we define black if

there was no white? How
about the concept of death
versus life, hard versus soft,
big versus little -- you get
the idea. We compare and
measure and thus begins
the separation process.

What if, instead of
looking at the opposite that
we perceive is there, we
look instead at the
similarities? What if we
truly look at how others
within our realm on this
Earth plane are "like" us?

Teri looks at a lot of
people because she's a big
fan of people watching.
Most of us are as it's kind of
entertaining at times,
especially if you go to
certain stores after midnight.
The thing is, though, to not
look at those that we see as

very different or separate from us but truly look at them, not with our physical eyes but with our spiritual or third eye. What a difference this makes! However, to truly be able to do this, we have to first look at ourselves this way.

When we look at our physical bodies, we can't see all of us at once unless we are looking at a reflection of us, right? What we usually see are hands and feet unless the belly gets in the way (oops, sorry).

The point is that we are seeing ourselves in pieces but not grasping that all those pieces, while individual parts, make up the whole person that we are. It's the same with the

Oneness. We are all just parts of this vast Oneness and we are all connected through Spirit.

What we are seeing when we look at another individual is the same as looking at our hand on our body. We are only looking at a part and not the whole. This is so hard to grasp because of our idea of contrast and thinking that we are unique and everyone else is different. They are not, trust me. We all came from the same place -- the Oneness.

Once we grasp this concept that we are all connected, we are all ONE; then it will be easier to make that spiritual connection to see, touch, and heal each other as well as ourselves. The connection is instantaneous once we let go of ego and look with our spiritual third eye. Everything before us comes into focus and we can identify imbalances and areas where the healing needs to be directed.

When we connect with the person to be healed, we do so from a fifth dimensional level. This takes preparation on our part, mentally, spiritually and physically.

The biggest obstacle to overcome, however, is letting go of the ego and realizing that our physical body is not doing anything other than moving out of the

way to let Spirit take over
and administer the healing
energy.

Chapter 3

THE CHAKRAS

The word chakra comes from Sanskrit and translates to wheel or disk, both of which bring to mind something that turns or spins. In the human body, chakras are spinning vortexes of energy which interact with and regulate the processes of our physiological and neurological centers. There are 7 main chakras in our bodies which govern our physical, emotional and spiritual functions including our immune system, emotional state and organ functions. There are more than the 7 chakras which are commonly known, including 5 sub personal chakras below our feet and 3 transpersonal chakras above our head (this number varies according to different sources).

What we deal with in TIME healing are the 7 main chakras along with the Earth Star chakra beneath our feet and the Soul Star chakra above our head.

ROOT CHAKRA

The root chakra is the first chakra. Its energy comes from the earth element and is associated with the feelings of safety and grounding.

Location:

The root chakra is located at the base of the spine, the

pelvic floor and the first three vertebrae.

Behavioral characteristics of the root chakra:

- Security, safety, survival.
- Basic needs (food, sleep, shelter, self-preservation).
- Physical identity and self-identification.
- Grounding.

In summary, the root chakra is all about the survival and safety, grounding ourselves into the Earth.

Root chakra imbalance:

- Excessive negativity, cynicism.
- Insecurity.

- Aggressiveness.
- Greed, avarice.
- Restlessness and sleep disorders.
- Eating disorders.
- Constant survival mode.

A blocked root chakra may turn into behaviors ruled mainly by fear, greed and paranoia.

Root chakra color

The color seen when observing the aura in the area of this chakra is red.

SACRAL CHAKRA

The sacral chakra is the second chakra.

Location:

The Sacral Chakra is located above the pubic bone and below the navel and encompasses the genital region.

Behavioral Characteristics:

- Emotions and feelings.
- Relationships and relating to others.
- Expression of sexuality, sensual pleasure.
- Feeling the outer and inner worlds.
- Creativity.
- Fantasies.
- Feeling of well-being.

Sacral chakra imbalance:

- Dependency, co-dependency with other

people or a substance
that grants you easy
access to pleasure.
- Being ruled by your
emotions.
- Feeling numb, out of
touch with yourself and
how you feel.
- Overindulgence in
fantasies, sexual
obsessions.
- Lack of sexual desire or
satisfaction.
- Feeling stuck in a
particular feeling or
mood.

Sacral chakra color:

The color seen when
observing the aura in the
area of this chakra is orange.
The orange of the sacral
chakra is translucent and
has a transparent quality.

A blocked sacral chakra will leave you feeling out of balance. A person may experience emotional instability including but not limited to fear of change, sexual dysfunction, depression or addiction(s).

SOLAR PLEXUS CHAKRA

The Solar Plexus chakra is the third chakra.

Location:

Located right above the navel area is the solar plexus which goes up to the breastbone.

Behavioral Characteristics:

- Both psychological and behavioral functions.
- Expression of your will.
- Personal power.
- Recounting everything you feel.
- Establish and manifest ideas and plans into reality.

Solar Plexus chakra imbalance:

- Excessive control and authority over people
- Helplessness and irresponsibility.
- Being manipulative.
- Misuse of power.
- Lack of clear direction.
- Lack of purpose or ambition.
- Lack of creativity.

Solar Plexus chakra color:

The Solar Plexus chakra color is represented by the color yellow. Since it is associated with the element of fire, it is also sometimes depicted as a yellow-red.

HEART CHAKRA

The Heart chakra is the fourth chakra.

Location:

The Heart chakra is located in the middle of the chest.

Behavioral Characteristics:

The Heart chakra affects our expressions of love and compassion as well as how

43

we relate to ourselves and others:

- How we give and accept love
- Ability to feel compassion and empathy
- Ability to see beauty in life
- Ability to forgive and accept others as they are
- Openness in relationships
- "Gut" feelings/insight
- Peace
- How we grieve

Heart chakra imbalance:

- Intimacy issues, especially with jealousy and codependency
- Isolating, nonsocial behavior

- Issues with forgiveness
- Stubbornness
- Defensiveness
- Envy

Heart chakra color:

The Heart chakra glows with a green hue.

The heart chakra can become imbalanced as a result of life experiences, physical ailments, or significant changes in your environment. It may manifest as a heart chakra blockage or an overactive chakra.

THROAT CHAKRA

The Throat chakra is the fifth chakra.

Location:

The Throat chakra is located at the center of the neck in the throat area.

Behavioral Characteristics:

The Throat chakra is our communication center. It is here that we voice our expressions, our truths, with both our "inside" and "outside" voice through:

- Speaking out and speaking up for ourselves and others
- Communicating by words and actions
- Creating, expressing our inner thoughts and bringing them to fruition

- Focusing on delivering messages received from Spirit
- Allow energy flow from upper to lower chakras and vice versa

Throat chakra imbalance:

- Inability to speak up
- Excessive fear of speaking
- Inability to listen to self or others
- Excessive or inappropriate talking
- Shyness
- Keeping secrets from others
- Gossiping
- Lying

Throat chakra color:

The Throat chakra is most commonly associated with blue as in turquoise or aquamarine blue.

THIRD EYE CHAKRA

The Third Eye chakra is the sixth chakra.

Location:

The Third Eye chakra is located on the forehead, between the eyebrows.

Behavioral Characteristics:
The Third Eye chakra is the center of intuition and foresight.

The Third Eye chakra is associated with the pineal gland which is in charge of regulating biorhythms, including sleep and wake time. This gland is located in the brain close to the optical nerves, and as such, sensitive to visual stimulations and changes in lighting. Characteristics include:

- Intuition, "knowing without knowing"
- Visualization
- Clairvoyance and clairaudience
- Creativity, insight
- Mystical states
- "Seeing" with your eyes closed
- Ability to communicate at multidimensional levels
- Out of body experiences

Third eye chakra imbalance:

- Lack of clarity
- Inability to visualize
- Rejection of everything spiritual
- Feeling stuck in a rut without being able to see a way out
- Fantasizing and believing illusions

Third Eye chakra color:

The third eye chakra is associated with the color indigo or bluish purple.

CROWN CHAKRA

The Crown chakra is the seventh chakra.

Location:

The Crown chakra is located at the top of the head or slightly above.

Behavioral Characteristics:

- Connection with higher consciousness, Spirit, higher dimensions
- Realization and freedom from anything that limits creation
- Allowing communication to flow from and to higher self/Spirit
- Ecstasy/blissfulness of spirit
- Awareness/clarity

Crown chakra imbalance:

- Feeling disconnected
- Cynical attitude toward anything spiritual
- Obsessiveness
- Closed mind

Crown chakra color:

The crown chakra is most commonly associated with the color violet or deep purple.

Chapter 4

CHI (QI)

Chi is the circulating life energy that Chinese philosophy has thought to be inherent in all things. It is life-giving energy which is believed to unite the body, mind and spirit. Chi is an ancient inner wisdom that has been forgotten by modern times.

Chi is also more than life-energy; it is a psychological power that engages your mind to find more possibilities on how to process and blend your energy into what is needed rather than forcing your actions into situations. Chi is not a superficial 'thing' but rather something that lies deep within us. It is a way to find the golden path, your spiritual path while working with you.

A strong life force will make a human being feel totally alive, alert and present whereas a weak force can result in sluggishness and fatigue. You can increase and develop your chi to overcome illness and become more vibrant. It also enhances your mental capacity.

The chi concept of life force energy is found in most ancient cultures in the world. In India, it is called 'prana', in China 'chi' and in Japan 'ki.' To the Native American it is known as 'the great spirit.'

Traditional Chinese medicine (including acupuncture) is based on balancing and enhancing chi to bring the body to a state of health. The concept of chi extends well beyond the physical body; it is the subtle energies that activate all human functions, including thought and emotions.

Each acupuncture point has a specific function related to the body. For example, the toes, ankles, knees, fingers, wrists and elbows contain these energy pools. When a symptom presents itself in one part of your body it can be alleviated via an acupuncture point located in a completely different location on the body. This works because the point being stimulated lies on a meridian whose energy fully passes through the injured portion of the body. This reference is made so that you will understand that the chi energy flows throughout every energy portal within our human frame.

Unbalanced chi will cause your emotions to become agitated or distressed whereas balanced chi will cause your emotions to feel more balanced. Balanced chi promotes higher states of consciousness.

Great strides can be made to not only direct the flow of chi, but to improve it with simple exercises and practice. When your structure (body) is aligned and in good posture, and your muscles and joints are relaxed, chi energy will flow throughout your body in an unobstructed, life-giving way.

Chi (Qi Gong) Healing can be utilized and witnessed in our daily lives. We witness the power of our minds to manifest and make things happen all the time. I am sure that some of you may wonder how anyone can be healed by applying a hand's on approach such as Qi Gong or even Reiki.

The same would apply to distance healing as both methods utilize life force energy to bring about the physiological healing to a diseased or unbalanced person. So, what does it mean to maintain the flow of chi?

Chi metaphorically describes your internal energy circulation. It means being connected and in synchronization with all things outside of our own being. It will bring you to a state of oneness.

Being in oneness means we are connected to the Universe, as we are not separate. Eventually through spiritual evolution you will become aware that we actually live in a never-ending cycle; as is the perpetual motion of the universe.

Our bodies consist of both spirit and essence. We are more than the human existence we now live.

Spirit and essence are interrelated. While spirit guides one's life, without chi we would lose all sense of direction. Therefore chi is all encompassing. Chi can also be developed and cultivated by working with Qi Gong exercises. Chi will not only benefit your physical self by doing Qi Gong exercises the life force energy will work together to improve and more deeply connect your psyche and spirit together.

We have a very integral matrix in our body. There are networks of meridians or channels through which chi flows, thereby nourishing and energizing the body. These channels form the matrix within our physical bodily functions. Along the path of these meridians there are places where our chi energy pools and may be more accessible than the other places.

Chapter 5

Archangels and Ascended Masters

We all have voices in our heads but how do we know if it's our ego, intuition or the voice of our spirit guides? They are too numerous to count. Thoughts enter in and out of our minds constantly either consciously or subconsciously. Let's look at how we can differentiate these voices. We are all born with an ego which is how we define ourselves as being separate and unique from others in our world.

We all have "ego speak" going on inside our head, feeding us information about survival, basic needs, fears, daily happenings and our reactions to them. This egospeak is highly influenced by those closest to us, by our society, by our experiences and our culture that we live in. While its main function is to help with survival, it has a tendency in most people to dwell in the lower vibration of fear and lack -- what we want, what is causing stress, causing us to look at things from a victim mode if these thoughts become prevalent.

The ego doesn't like to be challenged so when we hear something we disagree with or are in denial about, we react rather than respond at a lower vibrational level. You may know someone (perhaps yourself) who has made the statement or proven that the quickest way to get me to do something is to tell me I can't! Since we have free will, our egospeak always seems to trump the other voices. The ego is not tangible and is mindless but due to living in 3D energies for so long, it thinks it is in control. To some extent actually, it is, as we have allowed that to happen. We give away our personal power a lot.

We also receive communication from our higher-self. The higher-self is that part of us that connects us directly to the spiritual realm. Deepak Chopra calls this the "you inside of you." Eckhart Tolle relates that we all entered our human bodies from a higher dimension and left a part of ourselves in this higher dimension because the Earth energies are a lower vibration; however, we can at any time communicate with this higher-self. Many times the higher-self communicates without words but rather images or colors, sometimes even a "nudge" toward something (or away from it).

When we receive messages from our higher-self, they make sense. If you are hearing something that "doesn't set well" with you and everything in you is telling you it is false, then you need to listen to that inner guidance system because more than likely it is not coming from your higher-self. When we are open to our spirituality, we have the "knowing without knowing" and when our higher-self communicates, confirmations are made with this inner system of checks and balances and we are left with a sense of peace about it.

The Archangels

Most of the Archangels names end with an "EL" suffix. "EL" means "in God." The Archangels are able to be in many places at one time and you never have to be concerned that your problems are not important enough or that you are bothering them. This is why they are here and why they exist, to help us grow. While there are many Archangels, they surround us in peace, love and light. The most well-known Archangels are those depicted in the Christian Bible and they are Michael, Raphael, Gabriel and Uriel.

The Archangels protect and guide us and they just love us immensely. Their Divine power and wisdom inspire us to our highest good and highest potential, and because each Archangel is available at any time, to every single person, you would never need worry about taking them away from something more important. To these beautiful beings of light we are equally important, loved and guided. Not only do they bring personal support, love, comfort, wisdom and healing, they also function to bring healing light and love to Mother Earth thereby trying to bring peace on earth. At the time of this publishing we are aware of and communicate with 15 Archangels; however, there is a sense that many more do in fact, exist and that we will one day come to know them.

God has given all of us free will and the Angels and Archangels are not permitted to interfere with that unless we specifically give them our permission to do so. We know so many who have granted these beautiful beings of light permission to jump in and help us, not only verbally but mentally as well since if there is ever a time we cannot use our voice to speak we can telecommunicate. The Archangels see everything and every situation that goes on in your life, so you are able to discuss anything with them. Nothing is too small or trivial for our Angelic friends as they are here to guide us.

Before we discuss each Archangel you may ask, how do I connect or contact them? All you need to do is to call to them. You can simply say, Angel, I need your help. They always come when you call and if you open yourself up to their energy, you will come to know and feel their presence. The best way to communicate is to clear your mind and meditate, therefore allowing the energy flow. You do not have to force it to happen but you will need to clear your mind and let things just flow naturally. You can experiment and work with one Archangel at a time depending upon their specific role and what you may need at that moment. It would be a great idea to maintain a journal so that as you connect with the Archangels you can write down anything that comes to your mind. Bear in mind, communication is different for each of us, for some it is visual (in the third eye) where you may see images or colors; for others it may be just the feeling of a presence, whereas for others it can be audible. If you begin to work with one Archangel at a time, you will eventually have the ability to learn their specific energy, size and color of their healing ray. You will know how they sound, how it feels and even how they may smell, to you. With time and commitment on your part to meditating or freeing your mind, you will be able to deeply communicate with each one in a way that is easy for you to understand and comprehend. Their communication differs with each human being.

The 15 Archangels are quite well known. Their whole desire is to create peace and love. Please do not be fearful or unsure about calling to them. They will bless you with what you need and more than you may even realize or know since sometimes what we think we need is not really the answer.

The Archangels are extensions of God's love for us all, and as such, they do not want to be worshipped nor do they want us to pray to them. When you pray to God or even accept help from the Angels, one thing to bear in mind is that your gratitude is always appreciated. When we are grateful, we are given more to be grateful for, a little something to ponder. ... And so, without further ado let's discuss our beautiful Archangels.

Ariel

Archangel Ariel's name means "Lioness of God." Ariel gives us courage, bravery, and confidence. When Ariel is near you, you may begin seeing visions of lions around you. Ariel is also associated with the element of wind. Found in books of Judaic mysticism, Ariel worked closely with

King Solomon in conducting divine magic. Her energy color is a very pale shade of pink and her healing gemstone is the rose quartz crystal. She works very closely with people who are healers and teachers and she is very much interested and involved with environmental causes and issues.

Azrael

Archangel Azrael supports grieving and dying people. In both the Islamic and Hebrew religions he was known as the much feared "Angel of death." Azrael's name means "Whom God helps." He is primarily responsible to help people cross over at their time of human death. Azrael's energy color is a creamy white color. Azrael's healing gemstone is yellow calcite. He supports helpers, healers and counselors. He is known to be both very patient and compassionate.

Chamuel

Archangel Chamuel's name means "He who sees God." Chamuel works with and helps you to find the career best suited to your life's purpose and passion. Chamuel is known best as the Archangel of pure love and he can lift you from the depths of deep sorrow and despair. He will also heal and renew your relationships. Chamuel's divine energy color is very light pink color. Chamuel's healing stone is green fluorite crystal.

Gabriel

Archangel Gabriel's name means "Messenger of God." Gabriel has been depicted as both male and female energies; however, she is best known as the Angel Gabriel, the messenger who told Mother Mary she was to have a child. Call on Gabriel when you find your chakras need to be aligned. Her energy is very powerful. Gabriel will help you to overcome fear and procrastination, she motivates and works closely with artists and writers, notably known for dispensing the gift of automatic writing. Call on Gabriel if you find your body and/or thoughts are full of toxins and you need to be purified. She will appear when you are truly ready to proceed with your life's mission and she works closely with our Akashic records. Gabriel's healing stone is the crystal citrine and her energy is copper colored.

Haniel

Archangel Haniel is known as the sensitive Angel, not that she is meant to be construed as delicate as Haniel is quite powerful. Her name means "Glory of God." She is a nurturing mother who is able to care for you and create miracles in your life.

Haniel shows you how to live to your highest potential as she is very good at working with natural cycles and rhythms.

She will help you to develop your inner wisdom and intuition and she is a wonderful support to those who wish to develop their spiritual gifts. Her energy color is a bluish white color, similar to that of the moon. Haniel's healing gemstone is moonstone. Wearing or carrying moonstone can greatly amplify your connection to spirit.

Jeremiel

Archangel Jeremiel's name means "Mercy of God." One of his purposes is to work with souls that crossed over in reviewing their life before they ascend to Heaven. Jeremiel also helps the living make life reviews and better choices as he will deliver mercy when asked for. He helps you to act in a loving way toward others as he is supportive in helping you to treat others with respect and love. Jeremiel's energy color is a very dark royal purple tone and his healing gemstone is Amethyst.

Jophiel

Archangel Jophiel is a beautiful, loving and caring

Archangel. Her name means "Beauty of God." Jophiel has a distinctly feminine energy and her mission is to bring all aspects of beauty to the world. Work with Jophiel to guide you in regards to your personal self-care, including beauty. She works with us in our relationships and can fill your heart with gratitude and joyfulness. Jophiel also helps you clear away clutter in your spaces since she sees everything as beautiful, she can be very inspiring. Jophiel's energy color is a dark fuchsia pink and her healing gemstones are deep dark pink tourmaline and rubellite. Jophiel will bring peace into our lives.

Metatron

Archangel Metatron like Archangel Sandalphon is one of two Angels whose names do not end in "EL." This is because they were both prophets who lived such pious lives that they were rewarded with immediate ascension into the Archangel realm. Metatron is excellent at clearing your chakras. Since he walked in human existence Metatron assists us with getting our priorities organized. He uses the Merkabah geometric healing cube to clear away lower energies. This Angel does not play around, in fact, he is quite serious in that he is a strong presence and while he will help all of us, he works very closely with some of us at a deeper level. If Metatron decides to work with you he will only do so if he knows you will keep your commitment. He will push you at times to get things done but don't worry, he is a very loving entity. Metatron's energy color is watermelon pink and his healing stone is watermelon tourmaline.

Michael

Archangel Michael's name means "He who is like God." Archangel Michael is probably the most infamous of all Angels, as he has been sainted and has churches named after him. He is featured prominently in the Bible and other sacred texts.

Michael can help you to remember who you really

are. He blesses us with deep love and is committed to removing lower or negative energies away from us. He often prefers to communicate with you in your dreams. His chief role is to remove fear from your life. He can cut energetic cords that tie you to another person, just by thought and he has a process whereby he vacuums you out, meaning he removes all negativity, fear and anxiety from your bodies (mental, emotional, physical, spiritual) and your home. Michael has a very powerful persona, he is muscular and he carries a sword which is the sword of protection. He is always in 'defense mode.'

Archangel Michael's energy color is royal blue

mixed with royal purple. His crystal healing stone is sugalite which can help you channel his profound loving messages.

Raguel

Archangel Raguel's name means "Friend of God." Raguel is very well known for healing arguments and misunderstandings and he brings harmony to all situations. He will help you to attract wonderful new friends into your life. Not only does this Angel assist you with balance in your relationships, he will help you with your relationship with you, which is often the most difficult of all relationships. Raguel also oversees the Angels and

Archangels. His energy
color is dark pale blue and
his healing gemstone and
crystal is aquamarine.

Raphael

Archangel Raphael's
name means "He who
heals." Raphael has long
been regarding as the angel
of health and healing, call on
Raphael to heal most any
condition. His healing is
often very subtle but you
will know he is present
because sometimes people
feel or hear a gentle buzzing
of energy, or they see green
lights sparkling before their
eyes. Raphael can reduce or
eliminate pain stemming
from both short-term and
chronic health conditions.
Raphael also works closely
with Archangel Michael to

not only bring about health but to clear away stress and fear which truly are a major factor in our health. Raphael's energy color is emerald green. His healing stones are the Emerald or Malachite.

Raziel

Archangel Raziel's name means "Secrets of God." This Archangel seems to have magical qualities and he has a way of helping us humans work through the layers of ourselves until we become more focused. Raziel is also the Angel of clairvoyance and can assist you with reclaiming your personal power. Raziel can also help to dissolve any troublesome vows you may have made in previous lifetimes, such as vows of poverty or chastity or even self-sacrifice. Raziel will help you to recall any life lessons that your soul has accumulated through time. These are housed in your Akashic records .and he can turn these into usable energy in your present life's mission. If you do not want to suffer the effects of these vows in this lifetime, call upon Raziel to remove them. Raziel's energy color is the rainbow. Raziel's healing gemstone is the clear quartz.

Sandalphon

Archangel Sandalphon like his brother Metatron is one of the two Angels whose names do not end in "EL."

Sandalphon's name means "brother," in Greek. Archangel Sandalphon is a great messenger to carry our prayers through to God. He intercedes on our behalf continually. One of Sandalphon's roles is to determine the gender of a coming child and he is the patron to all musicians. Sandalphon can help you develop a deeper connection with God. He has a very gentle energy and will help you feel the love of God within and feel secure knowing that you are deeply loved and cared for. He can help you to live your life with integrity and allows healing to flow as he helps you to speak your truth. Sandalphon's energy color is turquoise and his healing gemstone is also turquoise.

Uriel

Archangel Uriel's name means "God is light." Uriel's chief role is claircognizance. He illuminates our mind with information, ideas and insights. He will work closely with you once you call upon him as he can guide you to your intellectual pursuits and is very good in helping students with their tests in school. This Archangel will whisper words or thoughts into your ear which you will receive sort of as a download of energy in your mind. Uriel's energy color is yellow and his healing gemstone is amber. If you wish to connect with this Archangel, be sure to carry amber with you.

Zadkiel

Archangel Zadkiel's name means "Righteousness of God." Not only can this Archangel help us to remember things, he will help teach us to comprehend new things and have access to all knowledge. He is a great healer of the mind who will gently guide you by the hand and help you take responsibility for your own happiness. Zadkiel's dual focus is on forgiveness. He can shift your focus away from painful memories in the past and direct you to live your Divine life purpose. He will help you to recall the beautiful moments of your life and he is wonderful for assisting with emotional healing. Zadkiel is known as the Archangel of clairaudience. His energy color is deep indigo blue and his healing gemstone is lapis lazuli.

The Ascended Masters

A lot of information and probably misinformation can be found both on the Internet and written in books about these entities who we have come to know as Ascended Masters. Some are very well known whereas others not so much but that does not make them any different because, you see, we are all part of the Oneness or Source of all that is.

There really is no hierarchy as some would have us believe. These wonderful Masters have revealed themselves to us out of love and where there is pure love, there is no room for the concept of "higher than" or more powerful than. In other words, there is no competition as there is no ego to be stroked. The ego is a human quality and these Ascended Masters, while they did exist in the physical, have moved beyond this realm and therefore have left ego behind.

Ascended Masters are believed to have acquired the wisdom and mastery needed to ascend to a complete and permanent union of their physical incarnation with their higher self and now operate at this higher vibrational level at all times.

When we speak of the Ascended Masters, there are certain terms that are commonly used:

- Chohan: Refers to an Ascended Master or Lord.
- Dharma: Divine plan.
- Dimensions: The realm in which we are vibrating.
- I AM: Refers to the Creator, Source, God, Divine.
- Initiation: The concept that there are 9 levels of spiritual development to progress upward to.
- Ray: A concentrated stream of spiritual energy. It is commonly believed that there are 12 rays representing the divine evolution of peoples and planets.

We are incarnated into one of the 7 rays (our soul ray) but are influenced in our lives by the other rays and can receive help from the Ascended Masters associated with these other rays.

Wikipedia lists the rays and the associated Ascended Masters as:

- 1 Blue (willpower, faith; material goods): Master El Morya (God's will), God Thor and Elohim Hercules
- 2 Yellow (discipline, intelligence): Master Lanto
- 3 Rose (beauty; genius): Master Roweena
- 4 White (ascension; peace; spiritualization): Master Serapis Bey

- 5 Green (prosperity; nature) : Pan and Hilarion
- 6 Pink (sacrifice): Master Jesus Christ, Master Virgin Mary
- 7 Violet (New Age, technology; transmutation): Master Saint Germain (Saint Germain).

- 8 Turquoise (clarity): Master Kenich Ahan
- 9 Magenta (divine miracle): Master Lady Magnus (South Pole) and Master Polaris (North Pole)
- 10 Gold (materializations of the riches): Divinity Gold and God Alexia
- 11 Orange (Nirvana): Master El Moriah
- 12 Opaline (renewal; rejuvenation): Lord Gautama.

Let's look at some of the Masters that have been revealed to us through history. There are many more but we will not list or introduce them all. We have chosen to highlight some of the more commonly known from each ray to help guide us but we do encourage you to explore the wealth of information available regarding these wonderful Masters.

Confucius:

Confucius (born K'ung Fu Tzu was a Chinese philosopher, teacher and leader who taught the virtues of kindness, wisdom, faithfulness and reverence. He serves on the second ray of Divine illumination, discipline and intelligence. Call on him to help you heal your internal wounds, beginning by being honest with yourself and for insight and wisdom in healing our great Mother Earth.

El Morya:

El Morya is another Master who has had many incarnations, probably the most famous of which was Abraham. He is associated with the first ray and therefore helps us not only to find our spiritual path but also helps in matters such as willpower and finding our inner strength.

Hilarion:

Hilarion is Chohan of the fifth ray, the green ray of

healing, truth and knowledge. One of his many incarnations was as the Apostle Paul, who showed great humility. The purpose of the green flame is self-reflection, self-truth and self-knowledge. Hilarion was a master healer. Call on him to help you heal yourself and to help administer healing energy to others.

Jesus:

Also known as Christ, Sananda, Savior, Yeshua and is perhaps the most well known of all the Ascended Masters. During his time on Earth, many wrote of his miracles that were performed to include healings and raising the dead, as well as his teachings which focused on unity with God. Call on him as Chohan of the fifth ray to reach a higher dimensional vibration and look beyond the physical incarnation to realize your true self as part of the Oneness and to understand and feel unconditional love.

Mother Mary:

Mother Mary represents the divine femininity. On Earth she was incarnated as the Virgin Mary, mother of Jesus. Call on her to help you take an active approach to spirituality, become self-sufficient and take responsibility for your life in all aspects. She can help you with inner reflection to bring you to a higher vibration. She is also the protector of women and children and assists in healing.

Quan Yin:

Quan Yin or Kuan Yin, whose proper name is Kuanshih Yin, is the embodiment of mercy, compassion and love. She helps balance the feminine energy. She also brought forth powerful healing energy. She is associated with the third ray of unconditional love. Call on her to help you find compassion and mercy for both yourself and others in your life and to find the meaning of pure love.

Saint Germain:

Saint Germain has had many incarnations including Francis Bacon, Merlin, Plato, Christopher Columbus and Saint Joseph. As Chohan of the seventh ray, he is well known for his violet flame for purification and transmutation of lower vibrational energy. Call on him to help clear your aura and remove anything in your energy field that does not serve your highest purpose.

Serapis Bey:

Serapis Bey is the Chohan of the fourth ray, the white ray of purity. He was incarnated as an Egyptian pharaoh, a priest of Atlantis, and a Spartan king. He is known as the great disciplinarian. Call on him to help develop the qualities of purity, hope, excellence and to help raise the Kundalini fire.

Chapter 6

THE HEALERS AND OTHER SPIRIT GUIDES

~*~ Spirit Guides ~*~

We all have voices in our heads but how do we know if it's our ego, intuition or the voice of our spirit guides? They are too numerous to count. Thoughts enter in and out of our minds constantly either consciously or subconsciously. Let's look at how we can differentiate these voices. We are all born with an ego which is how we define ourselves as being separate and unique from others in our world.

We all have "egospeak" going on inside our head,

feeding us information about survival, basic needs, fears, daily happenings and our reactions to them. This ego speak is highly influenced by those closest to us, by our society, by our experiences and our culture that we live in. While its main function is to help with survival, it has a tendency in most people to dwell in the lower vibration of fear and lack -- what we want, what is causing stress, causing us to look at things from a victim mode if these thoughts become prevalent.

The ego doesn't like to be challenged so when we hear something we disagree with or are in denial about, we react rather than respond at a lower vibrational level. You may know someone (perhaps yourself) who has made the statement or proven that the quickest way to get me to do something is to tell me I can't! Since we have free will, our egospeak always seems to trump the other voices. The ego is not tangible and is mindless but due to living in 3D energies for so long, it thinks it is in control. To some extent actually, it is, as we have allowed that to happen. We give away our personal power a lot.

We also receive communication from our higher self. The higher self is that part of us that connects us directly to the spiritual realm. Deepak Chopra calls this the "you inside of you." What we have learned from some of the great spiritual teachers of our time is that we all entered our human bodies from a higher dimension and left a part of ourselves in this higher dimension because the Earth energies are a lower vibration; however, we can at any time communicate with this higher self. Many times the higher self communicates without words but rather with images or colors, sometimes even a "nudge" toward something (or away from it).

When we receive messages from our higher self, they make sense. If you are hearing something that "doesn't set well" with you and everything in you is telling you it is false, then you need to listen to that inner guidance system because more than likely it is not coming from your higher self. When we are open to our spirituality, we have the "knowing without knowing" and when our higher self communicates, confirmations are made with this inner system of checks and balances and we are left with a sense of peace about it.

Now, about those spirit guides. This is different from communication from your higher self. The role of the spirit guide is just that -- to guide. It's that still, small voice that is sometimes whispered in our ear or that comes when we quiet our minds and ask to be spoken to. One school of thought is that we have one main guide that is with us from the beginning of our physical journey to the ending and on our return back to spirit helps with the transition. A spirit guide is different from an angel, although angels can help guide us as well. This is an entity (or entities) that have lived in a physical presence and have taken on the role of guiding (a guardianship if you will) us along our path. Our spirit guides are always loving and exude pure love in all their communication with us. They do not use fear tactics as their entire focus is on love and what serves our best and highest purpose. Not all communication from our spirit guides is verbal. It can be images and colors or a nagging thought. It can come through signs such as seeing a particular wording on a sign or shape of a cloud even. They may place things such as dragonflies or other spirit animals in our path.

We may see repeating numbers (111, 222, 333 ...). We may see orbs or lights or hear ringing in our ears. We may hear the line from a song and know that it is a message just for us.

I (Teri) will relate that for as long as I can remember, I have had a guide who communicated with me. I have always been aware of his presence but never gave him a name or even asked for the name. Yes, I was curious but it didn't really seem important. Just the fact that he was hanging around with me and allowing me to just be myself with him was enough. There were many times he shared things that came to fruition in my life. At times I listened and avoided some situations, other times not so much.

Whereas I (Rosanne) have a female spirit guide that has been with me since the beginning and who only in the last year finally revealed her name and gender to me, in deep meditation. I did ask for years for her name, I was a bit more curious than my partner. My other spirit guide is a male whom I knew very well in life, He was my biological Father who recently took on that task, with great pride. As he told me, I am new to this; I may make mistakes because I am after all still learning so please go easy on me! He always did have an awesome sense of humor!

It is interesting that the two who would be the founding partners for this healing modality had the opposing guiding forces -- masculine and feminine -- throughout their lives. There are no coincidences. Both the masculine and feminine are needed to magnetize the energy.

~*~ The Healers ~*~

It started with one, as does everything that has a beginning. It was in the channeling group "Teachings of the Masters" with Nicole Gans Singer that Joseph came forth as the first guide, revealing that his purpose was to help guide us through many difficult times and help walk us through the process of releasing and forgiving things that have happened during this and other lifetimes. The role of being lightworkers and healers is what Joseph is helping us to accomplish through this healing modality. In his incarnation in Egypt, he endured many hardships and thus understands that there are times when we want to give up, asking God why we had been dealt the hand we were given this lifetime, and always he encourages us to trust and lets us know that we were never alone even when we felt that we were. He teaches the meaning of humility and most importantly, he teaches us how to forgive. Without forgiveness, healing will not occur.

When the pupil was ready, the rest of The Healers revealed themselves as a collective. This happened in another channeling group with Joseph LoBrutto III where we were instructed to ask for the identity of our guides. Here, another masculine entity identified as Ben came forth and later was revealed to be Jeshua Ben Joseph (Jesus). His essence was so intense that his aura actually shone like gold. Pure love emanated from him. He revealed that he was known as a medicine man/ healer in his time as a physical entity with tremendous healing power.

That healing power is what is poured into the TIME healing.

Two feminine guides who were almost indiscernible as separate entities were next to be revealed as they were perceived as one, and held the essence of a twin flame. Immediately felt was the presence of Mother Mary as well as Quan Yin, two powerful Ascended Masters both bringing forth the teaching and guidance of unconditional love and compassion, so essential in the healing process. When TIME healing is administered, Quan Yin takes an active role in aligning and balancing the heart chakra.

With the balance of masculine and feminine energies in the collective, what was revealed next in the fifth entity was so amazing that it was revolutionary. This fifth entity, the nucleus of the collective known as The Healers, was indeed a collective within the collective!

So, to make this more clear, The Healers in every TIME session will always consist of the masculine and feminine entities as outlined above. However, they will be joined by numerous other fifth dimensional entities who will come forth to administer healing energy, depending on which TIME healer is facilitating the session.

Working as a collective, both the healing energy as well as attunements to the TIME healing will come through the facilitator and trainers.

Chapter 7

TIME

~*~ The Beginning ~*~

It has been said that everything is a manifestation of God. When something so powerful, so revolutionary is given in a thought form with specific instructions and imprinted into memory in a flash, in only a millisecond, it can only be attributed to one Source. Scientists say that our human minds have over 50 thoughts per minute and the average thought lasts only 3 seconds. When this information was revealed to Teri's human brain, it was done so while she was outside in nature and nowhere near a computer or recording device. This meant that the entire revelation had to be retained long enough to write it down and she was assured by The Healers that this would happen, which it did -- word for word as it was given to her.

~*~ The Test ~*~

Within days of the revelation of TIME, it was revealed that it should be brought forth to the world. This was something so huge that it took on a life of its own. A core group was formed of 7 people who Teri would lovingly come to refer to as the "Electric Company" as the energy was so very powerful in working with them. The technique was recorded and when reviewed by the recipients, verification was given that what was seen and felt was what was seen and given by the healer. Messages were coming through for those being healed. Among these messages one very crucial one was directed at Rosanne who was given an immediate attunement to the TIME energy and informed that she had been chosen to help bring this system to the world. Once the test group sessions were complete, it was then time to move on and start the training process to get TIME facilitators in place and spread the healing.

~*~ The Receivers ~*~

Specific instructions were given to those who would receive the healing.

One of the major components to TIME is that it is interactive; therefore, the person receiving was given a list of what to do at the very time they were being given the healing energy.

Instructions for receiving healing (DISTANCE):

1. At the agreed upon time, you will focus on being open to receiving healing energy.

2. You will protect yourself energetically with either a protective crystal such as hematite or black obsidian, and/or ask Archangel Michael to cloak you in a shield of protection so that only love and light can enter your field.

3.   You will give permission for the healer to connect with your higher self to participate in this healing process.

4.   You will hold one other person in your field of awareness to receive love and light while you are being healed.

5.   You will focus on the area(s) that are in need of healing and ask that your cells allow the healing to take place.

6.   You will focus on your breathing, breathing in the love, light and TIME healing and exhaling anything unlike love, anything that does not serve your best purpose.

7.   When you begin to feel the healing happening, you will pay attention to what exactly you experience and if possible write it down or record it afterward.

8.   Once you receive communication from the healer, you will release love and light into the universe by holding the intention for it to go out wherever it is needed.

9.   You will give thanks to your higher self, the angels and The Healers who participated in your healing.

10. You will provide feedback to the healer and identify any areas that you feel need additional attention so that both you and the healer can lift those

areas up to Spirit for healing to continue.

Instructions for receiving healing (FACE-TO-FACE):

1.   During the agreed upon time, you will sit comfortably and focus on being open to receiving healing energy.

2.   You will protect yourself energetically with either a protective crystal such as hematite or black obsidian, and/or ask Archangel Michael to cloak you in a shield of protection so that only love and light can enter your field. Your healer may choose to use a smudge stick also to clear the energy field of the room.

3. You will give permission for the healer to connect with your higher self to participate in this healing process.

4. You will hold one other person in your field of awareness to receive love and light while you are being healed.

5. You will focus on the area(s) that are in need of healing and ask that your cells allow the healing to take place.

6. You will focus on your breathing, breathing in the love, light and TIME healing and exhaling anything unlike love, anything that does not serve your best purpose.

7. When you begin to feel the healing happening, you will pay attention to what exactly you experience and if possible write it down or record it afterward.

8. Once your healing session is complete, you will release love and light into the universe by holding the intention for it to go out wherever it is needed.

9. You will give thanks to your higher self, the angels and The Healers who participated in your healing.

10. You will provide feedback to the healer, sharing any physical changes in pain/discomfort levels, spiritual insights or messages, colors, or anything that needs

clarification, as well as identifying any areas that you feel need additional attention so that both you and the healer can lift those areas up to Spirit for healing to continue.

~*~ The Facilitators ~*~

These very specific instructions were given to those who would facilitate the healing (the healers).

Instructions for giving healing (DISTANCE):

1. When you are ready to begin the session, you will hold the individual in your mind's eye.

2.   You will ask to be connected to their higher self to ask permission to administer the healing.

3.   You will enlist the help of their higher self, the angels, the Masters and your collective guides (The Healers) to administer healing energy to the recipient.

4.   After protecting yourself, you will scan their spiritual aura and bring in white light energy for cleansing the aura. (See the section following for protecting yourself)

5.   You will look for inconsistencies in the auric field where there is a lack or abnormality in the energy field.

6. You will activate your TIME healing by pressing first your left palm center while breathing for a count of 7 in, hold for 7, 7 out and then reversing to the right palm center and repeat.

7. You will begin at the Crown chakra of the individuals and scan top to bottom ending with the Earth Star chakra, again looking for areas that need healing and focus the TIME healing there, holding each area for a count of 7 in, hold for 7 and 7 out until all areas of lack have been dealt with.

8. Once you have reached the Earth Star chakra, pull energy from there and make a chi ball with it in between the palms

of your hands, bring it up to the level of the Heart chakra. From the Heart chakra, pull the energy of love and compassion and merge it with the grounding energy of the Earth Star chakra. Bring this ball up to the top of the recipient's aura field and pull in the energy of Divine love and spiritual connection from the Soul Star chakra to merge together in the chi ball. Pour this merged energy through the crown chakra and follow it down through each chakra center, then down the legs and out the feet going deep into Mother Earth and grounding the recipient with Mother Earth.

9. You will end by bringing the white light back up from the ground, bring the grounding energy with it

129

and pulling it over and around their aura, totally enclosing them in this ball of white light healing energy. You will then lift them up to the Universe, the angels, the Masters and the Healers for continued healing, sending them out into the universe, releasing anything that no longer serves them.

10. At this point, while you are still connected to the recipient and their higher self along with all the guides, angels and Masters, you will be still and listen for any messages that they want you to bring forth to the recipient.

11. You will give thanks to all that helped in this healing process.

12. You will contact the individuals when the process is complete and give them the information you gathered during the healing session. It is best to record it, either by video (preferred) or by audio and ask them to respond with any feedback to you and to let you know that they have completed their interactive part.

Instructions for giving healing (FACE-TO-FACE):

1. When you are ready to begin the session, you will clear the energy field with either sage or by use of crystals and salt so that only positive energy from Spirit can enter into

the auric field. You will protect yourself with either sage and/or crystals or any of the protective measures listed at the end of this chapter.

2. You will help clear their aura by use of either the comb method which is using your fingers to "comb" through the aura and removing anything that has attached itself that is not for their higher and best purpose. There are additional clearing methods, including calling in white light from the 5D realm that you may learn in the facilitator course.

3. You will ask to be connected to the receiver's higher self to ask permission to administer the healing.

4. You will enlist the help of their higher self, the angels, the Masters and your collective guides (The Healers) to administer healing energy to the recipient.

5. You will activate your TIME healing by pressing first your left palm center while breathing for a count of 7 in, hold for 7, 7 out and then reversing to the right palm center and repeat.

6. You will begin at the Crown chakra of the individuals and scan top to bottom ending with the Earth Star chakra, looking for areas of imbalance that need healing and focus the TIME healing there, holding each area for a count of 7 in, hold for 7 and 7 out until

all areas of lack have been dealt with.

7. Once you have reached the Earth Star chakra, pull energy from there and make a chi ball with it in between the palms of your hands, bring it up to the level of the Heart chakra. From the Heart chakra, pull the energy of love and compassion and merge it with the grounding energy of the Earth Star chakra. Bring this ball up to the top of the recipient's aura field and pull in the energy of Divine love and spiritual connection from the Soul Star chakra to merge together in the chi ball. Pour this merged energy through the crown chakra and follow it down through each chakra center, then down the legs and out the

feet going deep into Mother Earth and grounding the recipient with Mother Earth.

8.   You will end by bringing the white light back up from the ground, bring the grounding energy with it and pulling it over and around their aura, totally enclosing them in this ball of white light healing energy. You will then lift them up to the Universe, the angels, the Masters and the Healers for continued healing, sending them out into the universe, releasing anything that no longer serves them.

9.   At this point, while you are still connected to the recipient's higher self along with all the guides, angels and Masters, you will be still and listen for any messages that they want

you to bring forth to the recipient.

10. You can at this point ask for the recipient to provide feedback to their experience and their messages which were received. Note if there are any areas which need additional healing energy and if needed focus more energy there.

11. You will give thanks to all that helped in this healing process.

12. If you have the individual's permission, you can record the session, either by video (preferred) or by audio for them to play back at a later time and review what you were doing (some recipients go into a deep relaxed state during

the healing) and ask them again to respond with any feedback or memories to you.

~*~ Tools You Can Use For Your Spiritual Protection ~*~

Tools for our own spiritual protection are needed since the recent energy and DNA shift is in full-force. Many of us (ourselves included) have been under psychic attack recently.

What does it feel like to be under attack? Despair, depression, anxiety. You may feel very worried and often irritable or moody. Lack of self esteem and doubting yourself is another big indicator along with physical pain such as backaches, neck aches or headaches. You might also feel off balance or even clumsy. You question your existence and your spiritual journey. Admittedly, Kryon insists that we use these as crutches and they are no longer needed but I figure we have to do what makes us feel better for now.

There are specific tools we can utilize for our self-protection:

You can call on the dove which is a symbol of the Holy Spirit and it represents purity, freedom and things (situations) taking flight.

Of course you can always call on Mother and Father God, your Spirit Guides and Archangels.

Michael specifically is a warrior of truth and he defends us constantly.

Raphael is the great healer and he can pour beautiful liquid emerald green light into you for immediate healing. These two Archangels are who we call on constantly but we do work with all of the Archangels.

SOME POSITIVE THINGS YOU CAN DO:

Don't withdraw or isolate yourself from others.

Spend time in prayer and deep meditation.

Laugh! Laughter is the best medicine it will release negativity and bring you happiness.

Listen to music. Many messages come to us via music and from Sandalphon.

Expand and extend your Aura around you. You can demand that it expand outward and have it band together with divine light.

Cleanse and align your chakras every day. There are many wonderful videos available on the www that can educate you how to do this but also, Archangel Metatron is also a wonderful healer and he can do this for you as well as Archangel Gabriel.

Wear crystals as these also absorb negative energy.

ASK TO BE SURROUNDED IN DIVINE LIGHT:

The golden light of Christ consciousness.

The purple light of spirituality.

The silver Light calls in Azna in emergency situations.

Green Light for healing and prosperity.

Silver blue light to cocoon you in safety.

Afterword

Where do we go from here? Just because a person goes out and buys a set of pots and pans, that does not make them a chef. What you have been given in this book are the tools necessary to perform your own self-healing as well as to pursue becoming a spiritual healer using the TIME method.

Specific training in this modality is offered by the Angelspeakers, Teri and Rosanne. This involves an intensive training where the student learns the correct process of facilitating the TIME method, both receiving and giving, becoming familiar with The Healers and assuring familiarity with the chakra energy centers and how to align them.

There are attunements that are given from The Healers for the energy activation with each training session. Ethics is also covered as an important concept when facilitating the healing sessions. Support is always available even after the trainee is ready to perform sessions on their own.

If this is something you want to pursue, please contact either Teri or Rosanne through any of the means listed below at the end of this book.

BIOGRAPHIES

<u>TERI MILLER</u>

Teri Miller was born in a little town in Kentucky where she was in touch with spirits at an early age. She is a psychic, spiritual medium and spiritual healer who developed the TIME healing modality at the inspiration of her spirit guides, The Healers. She has led meditation groups in Florida as well as New England. She has held online meditations for people across the world, focusing on the Archangels. Many of her guided meditations can be found on YouTube. Teri also offers psychic readings, calling on the angels and spirit guides to assist.

Teri's diverse experiences which she terms "adventures" can be followed on her website at http://www.angelspeakers.com as well as on the Facebook group at https://www.facebook.com/groups/angelspeakers. She can be followed on Twitter @kygurlinaz.

Teri currently resides in Ft. Lauderdale, Florida with her two very intuitive cats, Tazzie and Gizmo.

ROSANNE LOMBARDO-HEATON

Rosanne Lombardo-Heaton is a psychic/intuitive, spiritual healer, Certified Angel Card Reader as well as a TIME healer and Reiki Practitioner. She has always felt that she had a higher calling and now that her professional career in the transportation industry is behind her, she dedicates her time to working with and helping people heal.

You can connect with Rosanne on her website: www.angelicinsightswithrosanne.com where she blogs regularly or on Facebook in her group:

https://www.facebook.com/
groups/earthangelsoflight.

Rosanne currently
resides in New York with her
husband Jimmy and their
two cats Maggie and Kiki.

DISCLAIMER:

Energy therapy is a natural method of energy balancing, but is not meant as a substitute for medical, or psychological, diagnosis and treatment.

Energy practitioners do not diagnose conditions, nor do they perform medical treatment, prescribe substances, or interfere with the treatment of a licensed medical professional.

Energy therapy or any other natural healing therapy should not compete with medical doctors and their treatments. All therapies are meant to complement medical treatments.

NOTES:

BIBLIOGRAPHY

Below are listed some of the books/authors that have influenced our lives in tremendous ways:

Archangels 101: How to Connect Closely with Archangels Michael, Raphael, Gabriel, Uriel, and Others for Healing, Protection, and Guidance by Doreen Virtue, published October 1, 2011

Autobiography of a Yogi by Paramahansa Yogananda, first published 1946

Change Your Thoughts - Change Your Life: Living the Wisdom of the Tao by Dr. Wayne Dyer-- published July 1, 2007

Journey of the Soul - Tools for Protection by Sylvia

Browne, published June 1,
2003.

Mother God by Sylvia
Browne - published February
1, 2004

Stillness Speaks by Eckhart
Tolle, published September
2003

Wheels of Life: A User's
Guide to the Chakra System
(Llewellyn's New Age Series),
published 1987

Other noteworthy teachers, authors and reference works are:

Brian Weiss

Dalai Lama

Deepak Chopra

Esther Hicks "Abraham"

Lee Carroll, "Kryon"

Louise L. Hay

Marianne Williamson

Rhonda Byrne

To contact a facilitator for healing or training:

Teri Miller:

Email
teri@angelspeakers.com

Website
www.angelspeakers.com

Rosanne Lombardo Heaton:

Email
Rheaton0517@gmail.com

Website
www.angelicinsightswithrosanne.com